VIA Folios 179

Colloquy on Mad Tom

Published by Bordighera Press, an imprint of the John D. Calandra Italian American Institute of Queens College, The City University of New York.

25 West 43rd Street, 17th Floor, New York, NY 10036

All rights reserved. Parts of this book may be reprinted only by written permission from the publisher, and may not be reproduced for publication in media of any kind, except in quotations for the purposes of literary reviews.

Library of Congress Control Number: 2025931154

© 2025, Matthew Cariello

VIA Folios 179
ISBN 978-1-59954-229-4

COLLOQUY on MAD TOM

Matthew Cariello

BORDIGHERA PRESS

for Michael and Norma Jean

Table of Contents

Garbage	9
Road Kills	10
Kestrel	13
Finding My Religion	15
The Cowbird	16
Crow	17
On the Great Wall	18
The Wreck of the "Lucy Evelyn"	19
On Water	20
Colloquy on Mad Tom	21
The Red Salamander	32
The Lilac	33
Tides	34
Solstice	35
Smoke	36
At the "Van Gogh in Arles" Exhibition	37
When the Dead Visit	38
The Yellow Notebook	39
The Words Not Included in This Poem	49
Sonnet on the Night John Lennon Dies	50
Mr. Hard Welcomes Me to GG White Middle School	51
Nancy & Me & the Men in the Moon	53
The River in the River	55
Nothing Falling	59
Pinking Shears	61
The Brick Path	63
Incident on West 4th Street	65

Short Days	67
The Mouth of the Sea	72
Fast Water Past the Cheese House	73
Acknowledgments	79
About the Author	81

Garbage

The machinery of the garbage truck delights me,
the whine of the gears, the strain of the engine

toward the next stop in the alley. I stand there,
amazed at the way the men who follow that truck

allow it to perform, the careful clicking thread
of the cable that lifts my refuse to the open cavity

that accepts all, that takes and takes again
without a single complaint. My left leg aches.

The spots on my hands are my mother's hands.
What's left of my hair is grey. I toss the bags

into the can. When the truck stops to gather
what's left, I gape in wonder by the gate, strain

under the weight that holds me up, stagger.

Road Kills

(Wayne County, Ohio, 1991)

At the end of the driveway
waits the first – its head
indecipherable among
matted orange fur.
I imagine the cat hissing

madly at the wheel
above him, and then faces
in the windows, pulling
at their shades all night.
Once out of town,

where the speed limit rises,
a possum, raccoon
and two squirrels
before I drive a mile.
The possum is new, naked

tail curled through its legs,
and clean, as if after dinner
it rolled over to sleep
and just didn't wake.
Beyond Wellington,

a rabbit on the railroad tracks,
then the goose I just missed
yesterday, feathers pressed
across a twenty-foot scatter.
Then for miles the road

is clear of flesh, though
stuttered skid marks
mark where a kill took place.
And somewhere hangs
a skunk's ozone.

Past Sullivan,
I look for the beagle
who swelled in the heat
then shrank and flattened,
and still no one came.

Or the spotted doe,
legs up in the ditch,
too far out of season
for even the poorest man
to drag her home.

Her legs buckled back
and she sank silently away.
Just before Polk
there's something bulky and black,
a calf with long knobby legs

crossed at absurd angles.
In a few hours, someone
will notice it missing,
but by then its rising belly
will be a total loss.

Where the Overton Road
joins the Killbuck,
where I pull hard right
against the slope of the road,
a woodchuck's carcass lies

crumpled on the center line.
Around that blind turn
last night some truck
surprised him, once so clean
and careful.

Humped beside him is another.
As I brake and swerve,
it leaves the ground
with quick and labored flapping,
barely flying, crawling up the air.

No crow, no raven,
no eagle in the road
would take its six-foot wings so slow
and hop the roadside ditch
to wait for me to leave.

I back my car and stare
into the cavity of the woodchuck,
picked nearly clean.
From my side the vulture rises,
rocks and tilts unsteadily,

then drops and swoops the car.
He claims for himself
what I can only leave behind –
the delicate refuse, the spiraling bones,
the knotted flesh gone dry with fear.

Kestrel

> *No thought of honor ever did assay*
> *His baser breast, but in his kestral kynde*
> *A pleasant veine of glory he did find.*
>   EDMUND SPENSER, "THE FAIRIE QUEEN" II.III.4

Crank of dusk, a leper's clicket,
in spring it rises above the rooftops,
skirts the cliffs on the western edge
of this city. On racketing wings
it rises and plummets, wings

stroking laterally, a bell's clapper
above the street noise. It draws
spirals in the air, whistles and follows
me where honeysuckle
sweetens the street.

Don't think I don't see it
there, over my shoulder,
flitting among thin wires of the sky.
All night it waits near the window
at the foot of my bed

and watches my sleep.
All night it calls to another
high above, calls to the moon's choir.
With a flourish, the throttling talon
raises hell across the mouse's back,

with wing thrusted surge
and bolted breath, it knows me
and fires my sleep. In a black
and cricketing factory
the articulate chorister keens.

Finding My Religion

Every poem is another moment of regret
for not having finished the last one; each day

an attempt to remain standing in spite
of the tidal bore forcing your mouth shut.

Sunday dusk filters through the windows, dust,
and trees. The house is empty but for wine

and a certain song that keeps coming back,
unbidden, every waking moment. Be careful

what you love too much. You're never alone
with the melody of your last life but relive

it with the tenacity of squirrels in the attic:
no way in, no way out. The sun sets, the clock

moves forward and all you've got to show
is an empty sheaf of white space on every page

you've written where nothing happens.
That, and a roof, a few dollars, and dinner.

The Cowbird

The cowbird's song masks her true intentions.
"Like water falling," my mother would say,

before the music in her brain dazed her words.
The cowbird sings to mark the nest

she's laid her egg – another's nest
because (as we were taught) she doesn't care

for her own brood, but leaves it to other birds,
who feed an open mouth same as their own.

The cowbird chick will grow and peck
and kill its nestlings. Fully fledged, it flies away.

Don't ask me how I know. I've seen things.
I've seen a crow rob a starling's nest, limp

chick in its beak; seen a hawk catch the crow,
seen feathers fall like water to the grass below.

Crow

There is no province but the liminal. Past
the thicket, a patch of grey. Before that,

green branches balance in the rain,
or not in the rain. Or not in the rain.

A chance crow stitches the patchwork shut.
Or maybe words fail and neither rain

nor branches nor grey patch remain.
Just the rain. Or sky. Please don't

think it matters where and when.
Silence grows as the crow glides through,

or a different crow, or the same in a different
direction. I could go on and on like this

forever, dodging rain among the branches,
on the wings of a crow – not a crow but a raven.

On the Great Wall

Rows of corn basking in the late summer
sunlight, every day is a death. I'm the small

hooded pilgrim in a Bosch landscape, roaming
west toward a woman I want to love but can't.

September in my hands, Dylan in my ears.
I'm alone on a bus in the Indiana night.

The bus has stopped in those rows of corn
for no reason. I'll come back when I'm older,

as the saying goes, but not much smarter.
Oh clock of love calculating the Great Wall

where I once wept, I want to be the weather
of all readiness. I have, I have, I have not yet

begun to live. I'm a hooded pilgrim in the night.
Love, absolve me of the need for love.

The Wreck of the 'Lucy Evelyn'

When is a clock? The face and the hands –
hour, minute, and that ticking bomb,

counting down infinity, one tremor at a time.
When a clock is a clock, a clock is three things:

on the one hand, numbers are hours;
on the other, the numbers are minutes by five,

so that 2 is ten, 6 is thirty, 11 is fifty-five;
and the terrible seconds, like Sisyphus on the hillside.

Therefore, the years I used to count by one
now I count by five, and beneath it the racing

drum of death. For fifty years, I watched the schooner
sail in circles in Little Egg Harbor Bay.

But in truth she wrecked and burned the day
after the day I last walked her sooty boards.

On Water

Trees are in the lake, the lake collects the trees.
My green canoe suspends the difference.

A steady glittering, the constant tap of waves
fluently pulling at the shore; my paddle dips

in time and again the mountain rises, shining
with green and trees. Upon mountain-echoes,

sparkling until now, beyond the unseen side.
The ridge, the sky, the voice, the horizon recedes.

Written on water, neither above nor below
the surface of the lake, neither in nor out of it,

neither lost nor found, neither forgotten nor
remembered, neither written nor not written

in iambs: I am I am I am I am.

Colloquy on Mad Tom
in Two Voices

                First, there's nothing.
                Nothing except you noticing
                there's nothing. Next,
                there's something, like tracks
                or sounds, something green
                or brown or red, but not enough
                to really make you wonder.
                Still, you think there's
                something besides you
                looking. What is it?
                Is it an it? Or still just me?
                It's at edge of the woods,
                pausing, blending in
                with the brush. When
                the background drops away,
                it's like seeing for the first time.
                It was always there.
                It's bigger than you thought,
                not as lovely as you'd like.
                Although at first you want to grab
                a harness and meet it halfway,
                you know you can't.
                Not that it'll kill you.
                It just doesn't care,
                doesn't need to be tamed,
                has no need for rope.

When the moose turns and stares
at something far away,
you turn, too. In that
turn, you lose the moose.
All that's left is swaying,
just a little steam in the air,
distant vibrations,
a vague sense of something gone.
That's when you think –
how awful to have a body.

The bulldozer moved ceaselessly, without thought,
deliberate, capable, efficient. I watched it
from a distance, watched it run and roar –
cold metal and hot oil. Each tree that toppled,
I felt it in my gut, my feet, my fingers.
All those trees that took half a day to cut
by hand, gone in minutes. No careful
circling, measuring the height, seeing
where it fell before it fell. No chainsaw,
sledge and wedge and pike. Just a crack
and a groan and the leaves shaking wildly.

When I take a tree, I honor the wood,
measure its age, considered its life.
I look for seedlings, copies of the first tree
scattered in the woods. When my chainsaw
lops the limbs, then cuts the trunk
into stove-length pieces, I sing in a small voice
the service I'm doing. The large blocks
scattered on the ground are a memorial,
and the heat I feel in my own limbs
is a premonition of the warmth this wood
will afford, and my sweat is like the steam
and smoke that will rise from the chimney.

But not today. The trees lay stacked
and strewn, backs broken, headless
warriors scattered in the mud.

        Although the snow lasts longer
        and the storm grows,
        and birches bend in the wind
        off the hill, shiver and roll
        as the windows rattle,
        I know as I watch how
        snow covers snow, I know
        what the roots are doing,
        the roots and tubers swelling,
        the dirt around them warming;
        I know they must know
        something, every year waking
        without wondering.

        Swatches, swaths, clumps,
        clutches, shocks – I see
        them spread in bloom and leaf
        on the snow-covered ground.
        I think the whiteness is a canvas,
        and raise my hands like brushes –
        here the lilies, here the hosta,
        there, in deep shade, a forest of ferns.
        A day before the turn toward
        spring, the earth's boulders
        emerge, swollen with moonlight.

Last winter, I'd stared at a two-day snowfall
as it kept coming on, the stretch of woods
still – and that was why I'd seen it:

a patch of moving water in the stillness,
vapor rising from the surface. Not snowmelt,
no stubborn puddle in the middle
of the trees. I knew it came from deep
beneath. In May, after mud season,
I'd cleared away the brush, and found
the ferns and small blue flowers. The water
was neither warm nor cool, and black and deep.
That night I dreamed of a cul-de-sac
and a stream, driving on the wrong side
of the road, of a body in the brush,
three clean stones, and a red salamander.
Then a child lost in the woods, a child
who wears my clothes and speaks a language
I can never understand.

        Green stubble in the snow patch
        by the wall, topped with mauve,
        yellow, pink and white –
        the first crocuses.
        Three sprays of sharp sunlight
        at the feet of three birches –
        daffodils. A stream of light
        green bishop's weed that spills
        down the rise by the path.
        A bending sea of blue and purple –
        irises beside the pond.
        Yarrow, crimson and indigo
        crowding the house.

        Mid-July, the black-eyed-Susans –
        star-burst, sun-burst,
        caught between the ebb
        and flow of the sun,
        morning's branches,

        evening's last gasp of light,
        the fruit of the mist,
        ancient amber come crawling
        from clay, the fire of stones,
        the harvest of dirt,
        the center of the earth
        illuminating the night,
        black eyes of the night
        illuminating the morning,
        the day you were born,
        the knowledge of death.

        As evening comes on,
        they luminesce, and I watch
        them long into the night
        as they sway in the cricketing dark.
        I imagine a field, a hillside,
        seen in the distance as a sign,
        a symbol, evidence of a life,
        a signal from another galaxy.

Crocus, iris, daffodil, day lily; Solomon's seal
and jack-in-the-pulpit; yarrow, malva, lavender;
and black-eyed-Susans, which ruled the garden.
It was like piecing a puzzle together, one flower
at a time. Yet the puzzle was never finished.

But sometimes I see it all. The line of trees
bounding the yard, the layers of flowers
carefully arranged on the hillside, the pond
in the evening, the pond in the morning,
the pond overflowing.
                      The abbot died, but
                      they didn't bury him.
                      They just put his body

in a room to watch it rot.
They take turns sitting.
Isn't that odd? They sit
and watch him rot.
The townies won't have it.
The monks don't pay taxes,
own half the mountain.
Now there's a rotting body.
They say it's a violation.
Tell me something.
What do you think they do
about the smell?
Do they burn incense?
Maybe they bring flowers.
They'll watch him rot,
then burn the body.
Why not just burn it now?
Haven't they ever seen ashes?

I can see it in the photographs,
motionless on the shelves.
My parents as children, then closer
and closer until they passed me
and disappeared; my brothers
and sisters, all on the same track,
all growing old constantly;
the family of my wife, scattered
to the corners of the earth so that
no one photo could contain them all;
my own children, the son now too far
away for him to know what to say,
and the daughter, dead so many years
I'd lost count. And then the weight
descends. I leave the room,
try the next one along, or the hall,

see her face as a child, her face
as a young woman. Then her body
on the gleaming table.

                    I'd taken them all that day,
                    one by one by one,
                    digging a hole in the sky
                    where before had been light.
                    They were strong and fresh,
                    solemn in their resistance
                    to the cull, but succumbed
                    anyway, my clippers snapping
                    each lovely neck. I took them all,
                    at first counting to a hundred,
                    then knowing how useless
                    to keep going, but I kept going.
                    I took as much beauty
                    as I could from my sight
                    and gave it back to my child
                    beneath the closed door
                    to the other side. And they
                    became her face, the face
                    of her face, etched in
                    common black-eyed sunbursts.
                    A rough silt of ashes sits
                    on the mantle, body and flower,
                    distilled to their simplest
                    dusty, hoary essence.

Like twenty men working, the machine
had gouged the earth and made it tremble.
The machine that wrecked, the machine
that built, the machine that dug the holes,
the machine that dug the roads, the machine

that assembled the machines, the machine
that broke them down. It didn't stop to think.
It didn't ask why. It didn't stop running
even when it stopped running.
The hand is machine. The arm machine.
The body machine. The arm machines hand,
the hand machines the axe, the axe machines the tree,
the tree machines the stove, the stove machines the house.
I am a machine, I machine my own.

                      A solid month of satisfaction,
                      watching long and hard
                      as the first small flower came,
                      exploring for the others,
                      making sure it was safe.
                      Then the large, beckoning blossoms
                      that shot up on their strong stems,
                      a hand's width across,
                      too strong and too beautiful.
                      Then there were thousands.
                      Then a stasis, a time to languish,
                      a held breath, a skipped heartbeat.
                      After that came the gradual decay,
                      a slow descent toward the first frost.
                      The petals withered and curled
                      like brown fingers. Soon nothing
                      would be left but the black eye
                      at the center, dead and dry
                      and hard to touch.
                      With the first freeze,
                      the leaves would collapse,
                      and the once-lithe stems
                      would stand stiff and straight
                      and brittle in the rain.
                      I let them fall

       under the heavy snows
       until there was no trace
       of any burning flower.
       Only the white canvas –
       the blank face of winter.

The hillside was silent. I walked the perimeter
with my best tool, surveying the wreckage.
A dozen earthly lives, a dozen set of arms,
mouths with nothing left to say.
As the diesel drifted away, the engine
ticked loudly as it cooled: burnt oil and grease.
I ran my hands over the rusted
yellow paint, examined the gearshifts,
knobs and levers. The water was flowing.
I looked closely at what had happened,
then stepped in up to my knees.
I let the axe drop like an oar in a lake,
until it struck dirt. I kicked down
on the tool, kicked up a small load of mud
that slipped and clouded the clear water.
I did this again, breaking the surface
with my axe, then stilled and shook my head.
The water was rising. Nothing would stop it now.

            Just before dawn, the Buddha
            came to my garden, stepping
            carefully among the clumps
            of last year's close-cropped irises,
            among patches of remaining snow.
            I thought it almost clumsy,
            the way he'd plant his foot,
            ball first, and twist it slightly
            from side to side, digging

in to gain his balance,
then raise the other and step
over an iris leaf. He seemed
to be walking back and forth,
not looking up as he went,
and every few steps he bent
all the way over to inspect
a new shoot coming
from the ground.
Each time he bent, he exhaled
sharply, nearly mournful.
In his hand he carried a small lamp
where a candle sputtered,
although it gave scarcely enough
light to see. It was more like the light
on the prow of a boat.
With each awkward step
the lamp swung wildly,
a faint arc of light spinning about,
falling sometimes on the trees,
sometimes on the ground,
sometimes on Buddha himself,
who was sweating hard,
steam rising from his shining body.
He turned toward the house,
but his eyes rose higher,
over the roofline above me,
away toward the east,
searching for the sunrise.
His lamp shone bright yellow
on his face, though his eyes
were in deep shadow.

He was doing his dance,
for I saw it now as dance,
among the sprouting plants –

and I laughed when I saw this,
but caught my laugh and clapped
a hand to my mouth,
for he had spun all the way around
and laughed in return.

The Red Salamander

You can't find them. Then one is there.
The way you see is the way you see you see.

I'm upset by words and how they scratch
to be let in, by the twists of the story itself.

The red shadowed leaves, on the walk
or grass, begging for currency. Or how

we found the fiddler Alex three days running,
once up on the bridge in the park, once below,

then busking in the subway by the museum.
And you, my soul, as Whitman said, filament,

filament cast from the ceaselessly musing spider
that carefully crafts the flex that opens the mouth

singing, singing, singing, singing, singing –
the red salamander flees the burgeoning wood.

The Lilac

When my sister died, our mother cried *Why
won't God take me in her place?*

I collected lilacs from the roadside, thick
with bees, and left them on the table –

the desperate distillation of being alive.
And while we're here, oh God,

why, may I ask, did you ever let her die?
To prove our lives a futile gesture, to reproach

our wish for a future safe from simple suffering?
Do you really think I'm that stupid? We climb

the garden wall, think that the lilac that blooms
each spring means more than lilacs

bloom each spring. Don't ask me what
spring means. I don't know. The lilac blooms.

Tides

I left warm home behind the brush and roses
to listen to the muted rumbling, and feel heave,

buckle and rip as waves wracked the shoreline,
combing water into cords of light. I wanted

to know where the ocean goes when the tide
pulls it from the broken shore. A plover sang

in the sea-oats, but those minor notes didn't rise
to meet the moon. An air conditioner whined,

a telephone peeled back the dark. A neon sign sang.
Stevens was wrong: the singer that once strolled

that strand was gone, tracks sunken in the breach
between repetitious ocean and continuous shore.

Beyond the dunes, the sea's chasm slid open.
The ocean rushed in, hesitated, and was hidden.

Solstice

The solstice tastes like black berry brandy
or homemade beer, thick with flecks of yeast

and detritus of rain. *I should like the way this tastes*,
but don't. Chiaroscuro of trees and snow

in twilight. Radiators steam and clink.
The rice pot boils over. The clock has

stopped that ticked yesterday so well. The meal
is almost done, the family gathers. What if

someone asked, thirty years ago, under another
mackerel sky, where today would be? Could

you have known about waiting in the kitchen,
blackberry and beer, the pulse of the year fading,

standing staring alone in the gloaming, praying?

Smoke

Everything is known by the red thread of being.
The leaves sing spring, already bending

in the breeze that won't last, tempering
winter among the frozen roads home, expecting

the next season already, even while blooming.
What's beyond the first love, or lust, or false love,

remembered in winter's frame? That long
walk home in frozen stillness, tasting her lips,

the songs that played still playing – it hits you:
it never stopped starting, was always ending.

This is how Vincent left his life behind.
This is what I've been saying all along.

Imagine bees and blossoming wood smoke –
bees circling woodsmoke circling bees.

At the "Van Gogh in Arles" Exhibition

(1984)

The crowds milled the labyrinth looking
for a sign or symbol of their decision to look.

And I wandered as if it were a revelation
which drew us together in a sense

of anticipation and helplessness.
See the imbrications of straw and grass

spun around the slenderest saffron twigs?
May those delicate broken branches bend

slowly to the ground beneath my weight, may
(the patchwork of corn and wheat, brush strokes

of a man in a hurry, a ruptured geometry,
stone walls punctuated with red dots (flowers?)

two low clouds fade left to right from white
to blue, so they never touch) they lift me up.

When the Dead Visit

You're not how we remember.
You stare at running water,

glare at a spoon's glitter,
open all the cabinets.

You're careful where you step,
trip around the house, tipping vases,

tilting pictures, turning off lights at dusk.
You weep at wilting flowers.

"How odd to be that supple,
when I've become so brittle,

unable to slip below the sill,
under the black earth beneath the puddles.

Look at this body, how it floats
with knowing more than is useful

in this house. Beautiful because it leaves us.
Remember that song? Remember?"

After a few hours, we wonder why you're here
at all, wonder why the day won't pass.

The Yellow Notebook

In memoriam, David Ignatow

THE RESULTS ARE IN

There is always the possibility
that this is just a test.
Firecracker, gunshot–
quick, decide, react appropriately.
Then get another beer.
Right or wrong
doesn't count. The sun sets
(vermilion or sienna?).
The sun rises, but a day earlier.
In the end, I expect to find myself
in that first patch of city light,
where the shadows blinded me.

TOO SHORT

Sometimes I wonder
if I'm still alive.
Maybe everything
has already happened
and this life of mine
is simply unspooling thread
piling on the floor.
Someone comes
to measure, cut, measure

again, pack it in paper bags,
and sweep up what's too short to count.

WITHOUT ME

Racing my daughter down
long street, half afraid
she'll fall, half afraid
she'll pass me and
take what's hers.
Her easy strength
is frightening.
My legs falter,
my heart sobs in my chest,
and for one moment, exhausted,
laughing on the lawn,
I see her future clear
and long without me.

THE HERON'S NEST

This is how it works.
The heron's nest,
a crazyquilt of sticks and grass,
and the heron herself,
one tree away, ignoring
everyone and everything,
preens her crown of feathers.
If the nest is empty, she won't say.
I've never had a plan in my life.
Okay, maybe one or two.
The heron's beak is sharp as knives.

THE FIELD

Another day.
The jay wakes noisily.
Bitter coffee and sweet milk.
The deer grazing
near the airport
make me unreasonably happy.
They don't even look up
as the jets boom overhead
and the semis roll by.
One day I'll pull over,
enter that field,
and walk among them.

A POEM THAT IS ITS OWN TITLE

Standing in a fog
in New Paltz, New York,
listening to the distant
report of rifles,
I think of the skull
and the hide,
the meat of the thighs
and black broken hooves
I found scattered upstream
from where I had just
drunk my fill.

ROOT CANAL

The problem's in the nerve.
It senses pain that's
not there, imagines damage,
or remembers it from some harm

years before. The only solution
is to remove it, and once the root is gone,
there's no pain because nothing's left
to feel the pain. And it works:
not that there's nothing
to feel, just nothing to feel it.
In this manner, a whole mouth
can be repaired, and with it
will come a satisfying silence.

USEFUL QUESTIONS

To begin with a line
from Neruda,
"How many questions does a cat have?"
Please discuss
amongst your selves.
That's enough.
I'd like to say
you have just engaged
In an epistemological exercise.
Now I'd like to
show you the door.

CLOCKS

Dear Ko Un,
Wisteria in the rain,
deer at the meadow's edge.
Black-eyed-susans
before they bloom.
Absent hummingbirds.
The name of the tree.
Things I'd die without:
Clocks, scissors, pens.

What? You don't need clocks?
But I thought you said you did.

AGAIN AND AGAIN AND

Again and again,
like Sunday mornings
when I first learned to read
lying on the living room floor
sleep still in my eyes.
Comics, sports, then
the rest of the world
stacked in folds of newsprint.
Again and again
reliable mornings, familiar birds,
the unfoldment of words.

FATHERHOOD

All things matter
until they don't.
The finch's nest in the eaves
of the porch — its five eggs
must become five fledglings,
the five fledglings
my daughter guards
from the neighbor's marauding cat.
Then the fledglings become birds,
indistinguishable by the hundreds.
And my child,
she goes inside.

ANOTHER RIVER

I'm not making this up.
Rivers run inside me.
Hackensack, Pascack,
Raritan, Cuyahoga,
Battenkill, Hopmeadow,
Scioto, Olentangy.
The two-hearted Hudson.
Those are the ones I can see.
Others, deep inside,
run dark below the surface,
filled with blind white fish.

UNTITLED

3AM post thunderstorm:
My grandfather, toothless,
20 years out from his first heart attack,
and my sister, 3 or 4,
in the car beside him.
They're going to feed the ducks
near the pond in spring.
Nothing bad happens. A duck
eats bread from her hand.
Nothing bad happens, even though,
by the time I remember this,
they've both been dead a quarter century.

ANOTHER RETURN

And now the monarchs
with frayed wings
covered with the dust
of a thousand miles there,

another thousand back,
all just to return
to the same patch of milkweed
where they were born, nudge
the next generation to life,
fold their wings and die.
How beautiful the grass beneath my feet.

SWARM

Why not just insist yourself
into being?
Why not answer that koan
with a koan of your own?
What is this?
My bones lie in silence,
but my skin still crackles and hums.
The fire burns but flames
don't consume me.
What is this?
You mean, right now?

MY BOOKS ARE IN BOXES WAITING

My books are in boxes waiting
to be moved to other boxes
waiting to be moved
to other rooms, which wait
to hold them. After that,
who knows?
It starts again,
this constant relocation
of the moment that box
is opened in another room,
another box, another book.

THE RUNNER

Every step is a step
closer to pain, he says,
sweat flying from his fingertips.
What do you run from? I ask.
That same pain, he says,
slowly pulling away from me
in the heat.

SAVING DAYLIGHT

In the six minutes left
of daylight savings,
what can I carry
from one time to the next?
What will I save
when across America
this real thing called time
becomes this fake thing called hours?
What are years?
For all you know, I've thought
as much of you as you of me,
said Uncle Walt. In old houses,
do mirrors see the dead?
The older I get,
the more I hold with Ignatow,
who believed a poem
is a knife that guts sentiment.
So I parse and trim,
starting with the extremities:
lop off a limb, crop the shoulder.
I move to the head,
admire the tongue,
then toss the whole skull away.
Soon there's nothing

but fragments. *Now we're getting
somewhere*, he laughs,
hands me a needle and thread.

APPLE PICKING

What do I remember?
What do I imagine
I remember?
Each morning over tea
another song bubbles up:
summer 1973, searching the dial
all day for "Riders on the Storm,"
and now I can't lose it.

After apple picking,
20 pounds in the trunk.
Then the quiet ride home thinking
"20 pounds?"

CLOUDS

Let's review.
What is the meaning of what?
How is that spelled?
When is this going to end?
Where will these thoughts go?
Why, in the course of the course,
have I managed only one grade,
and that, an unknown letter?
Clouds above the hills,
hills below the clouds.

SOLSTICE SONG

Someone's taken down
the missing dog sign,
and the cicadas' first song and
the afternoon moon –
pay attention to how
a hawk circles the field,
and places where deer
have gouged the trail.
Remember your first
fatherless father's day?
The unseen heron's
unheard call,
the first monarch
and the last lily,
the limp life a skulking
cat carries in its jaws –
across a wide road
strangers call my name.

The Words Not Included in This Poem

The self is no-self, but mostly a corpus of
attempts to construct a self. The chasm's in the

loss of rock the water takes, but down which
darkened gorge? Maybe *I* is a pastiche, maybe

this isn't my life, and I'm really living in a
Manhattan flat with three cats and six sofas.

Some words, I think, fail to mean anything.
This sentence, for instance, is about everything,

but then again, it's not. This sentence has five
words. This one has four. This goes without saying.

This is true. This is easier said than done. This
is Tuesday. This is a death sentence. This is

context. This spells word. This final sentence
is only a sentence while you are reading.

Sonnet on the Night John Lennon Dies

It's December 8, 1980, and I'm up late
typing in the apartment of a girl I won't
marry and it's almost my birthday and
it's large and loud and electric and thumps
angrily when I hit the return key so it sounds
like someone knocking at the door, and even
though we won't marry, I take it as a sign
and head up the steps to where she's sleeping
but something makes me stop and turn

on the radio and there's nothing but Beatles
for some reason and all the stations are the same
so even though I might wake her and maybe
because we'll never marry I sit myself back
down and just keep hitting that return key.

Mr. Hard Welcomes Me to GG White Middle School

(1972)

My father's rusty Chevy rumbled
down Liberty Hill and stopped
in plumes of blue smoke at the
edge of the curb. He smiled.
"Today's the day, son, today's
a new day." Across the green
expanse of lawn, a door stood
open to the gym, and at that door,
a hand beckoned. I remember
the thud of the car, the soft
crush of grass beneath my sneakers,
the stink of fresh paint and tar,
the huge shadow of the building
stretching out to meet me. Inside
the gym it was silent. I was late.
But the man at the door stepped
across my path. "You," he said.
"Why did you walk across the grass?"
I stared down at my wet feet. "Go
back and enter correctly." I looked at
him, then gazed behind at how the
green was bent toward my path. "Back
over the grass?" I said. "Smart ass," he
replied. I wept as I laughed as I trotted
back through that vast lawn, found

the hard path, returned to the door,
and beneath his watchful eye
stepped into that new day.

Nancy & Me & the Men in the Moon

(1969)

The summer I was ten
I loved Nancy and her
rough round voice
and boy's haircut. She
lived across the street
and her father died
of cancer in the living room
three days after I
watched him eat two
bowls of corn flakes
while me and Nancy
played checkers on the floor.
He even drank the milk
in the bowl and smiled.
He went ahead and died
anyway. Nancy wasn't sad:
her father's pain was done.
We rode our bikes down
the big hill and pushed them
back up. We caught fire flies
and kept them in jars.
She had the only
blue house on the street.
Next door was Mr. B and
his wife Tootie B. They
had no kids, but let us
visit for soda, cookies

and color TV. That day,
Tootie swirled her afternoon
highball while Nancy
and I lay on the couch
in the dark, cool den.
We didn't talk.
We didn't hold hands.
We didn't even touch.
Just sat and stared at
far away ghosts of men
dancing on the silver surface
of some other planet.

The River in the River

> *The coin lost in the river is found in the river.*
> ZEN KOAN

It begins as rain,
insistent on the
roof, and reminds me of
another rain, another
year, and so becomes
the desire not
for rain, but that memory.
This is how it works:
rivulets collect
around my feet,
sluice toward the lowlands.
Soon I can't help myself.
The new rain is the old river.

*

Say that memory is a river,
but, like the Hudson,
it flows two ways.
Say that eight miles
the current takes
in southern descent,
the tide returns seven-and-a-half
in counterpoint.
Say that what's lost is
not lost, say that

telling and re-telling
tells the truth.

*

There's always a river.
I've seen it for years, ever
since a sunrise split the land
and left me on another shore,
already remembering that shore.
It's fast where the land is steep,
slow and wide among the plains,
bends back on itself
in oxbows of logic. Always
the river that speeds away from now.
Always that river.

*

In dreams
I can breathe
water, swim waves freely,
float effortlessly,
like a sea-turtle.
But when I see that river,
break its rough glass,
wear it in my hair,
it disappears.
The river can't bear
the mask of my joy.

*

I found her missing shoe
balanced at the edge of the gutter
on the corner where she died.

The gutter led to the sewer,
which led to the river.
The river will find me
when I stop trying,
but that's only half of it.
Am I ready to take the river
and take it nowhere? It is cold
and a hundred times bigger.
I must sit in the middle,
filling it.

*

Maybe memory is an accomplishment,
as Dr. Williams said, *since
the spaces it opens are new places –*
the river is when the words
fill the space between then and then.
Or has everything already
happened, and my life
is something other
than my own, and that's why
I can hear waters
deep beneath me
endlessly rolling.

*

The river flows in all directions
rippling, unbroken.
I'm awake, not so warm as I like,
but feeling my body's blood
sift through rock beneath the surface,
maintaining my balance from moment
to moment, and so, completely.
The serpentine song rises in a beat

that makes time and keeps time,
yet misses the movement of my breath,
and it's almost what I meant to say.

Nothing Falling

When school was over,
when the summer began,
when I left my friends and books
and the cafeteria's sad smell,
I'd wander the county, follow

my bike wheels through the woods,
past the parking lots in town,
searching. There were streams
below bridges, damp thickets
by the sandpit, the field

behind the school redolent
with queen-Ann's-lace,
and the birds in that field.
Let's count them and name
the names my mother said.

Cardinal, robin, jay, crow,
unseen owls and flocks of sparrows,
finches, chickadees and
endless endless starlings.
At the edge of the ball field

where I'd played baseball badly,
behind the stands, nearly
at the street, a moment of doubt.
I'd never seen this bird before.
It was nothing I'd ever seen.

It was far from home.
I knew the summer
was already over. I knew
it was going to end.
Already there were so many

things I'd never know.
Before that bird, there was only
breathing and beating wings,
but since that day on the edge
of the wood on the edge

of the field at the edge
of the summer, the breast
and the beak, the fluttering
wing and spiraling coil,
the banking turn, the flash

and lash of color at the top
of the turn through the leaves
at the top of the tree –
since then there's been nothing
but falling light and nothing falling.

Pinking Shears

Because there are more ways
to shuffle a deck of cards

than there are stars in the universe,
my mother leaned over the wooden table

with her black-handled pinking shears
and traced the outline of a Vogue pattern

she'd pinned to the fabric.
Why the zig zag? I asked,

listening to the meticulous movement
of the scissors, the thrum of the cut

through the wood of the table, each stroke
separating what was from what is.

So the fabric doesn't fray,
she said. The little strings,

they hold together, won't unravel
if you cut them right. I didn't yet know

what I didn't know: the way everything
is sprung with a seam on the verge

of slipping, how we're bound invisibly
to chance and accident. Let me see

the pattern emerge through the oblique
lines of the shears. Let me see the way

edges that bleed but don't tear
make something new and useful.

I have no idea what she was making.
Just the vibrating drum of the cut

resounding through the wood of the table –
a song that's the sound of stars,

dealt seriatim, burning, then flickering,
then fading, always out of time.

The Brick Path

From abandoned homes,
battered warehouses
flattened with fire,
from piles of rubble
on outskirts of cities where
"no dumping allowed" don't matter,
from the gasoline soaked
garages of immigrants
from the city, the children of
children of immigrants
from Germany, Italy, Ireland,
from broken roadside trucks
left in the Meadowland's high grass,
from the Turnpike, from Tonnele Avenue,
the Pulaski Skyway to all points west,
from the Hudson to the Delaware,
from get a job to get lost,
my father gleaned bricks,
never bought a single one,
gathered bricks by the bucket,
from Weehawken, Hoboken,
from the Palisades' shade
to the dockyards of Jersey City,
Paterson Plank Road to Moonachie,
the Chevy wagon bought for a hundred bucks
sagging on its springs,
hauling loads into the new world,
where the piles of bricks grew larger

until one day it stopped,
and he lit a cigarette
and surveyed the mounds,
saw how each brick was just a little different,
burnt clay, sand lime, fly ash, concrete,
each bearing the names of the dead
who made them (Rose, Sage, Shale,
Terry, Toppin, Tuttle, Wall)
cracked red, pocked orange,
and one whole pile stained lavender
by who knows what or who,
and he knew
that rebuilding all that was ruined
was simple work compared to collecting
that which was wrecked,
because once you had it, just lay it flat
in any direction you like,
build a curb, build a wall,
build that path back to the city,
build the city again, and he thought
what's the worst thing could happen?
My father never bought a brick, not one.

Incident on West 4th Street

(1983)

I was stopped in traffic on West 4th Street
and she approached my car of all the cars
in the Village that night (an ancient VW
with rusted out headlights and a wide hole
in the floor) and gently tapped the window
(which I rolled down) and asked in the nicest
blonde voice ever if I wanted a date
holding my eyes for a good five seconds
with her blue eyes that let nothing in or out
and did I want a date that could be anything but no kissing.

My first thought was why me in this car of all
the cars on the street why pick this one
we're all not going anywhere and the man
in the Beemer is more likely to say yes than me
in my dirty yellow Bug with the rusted out headlights
and a hole the floor through which I can see and smell
West 4th Street.

Did I mention I was a young man back then?

She had a pony tail and a face out of Botticelli
and a backpack and slim white hands
and smiled with perfect teeth and said she'd
fuck me for money and all I could think of
was my dirty car with the hole in the floor through
which the wet pavement of West 4th Street shone.

So I smiled back at her eyes that let nothing in or out
but were wide and lovely and bright in the rain
and in my small soft voice of shame said I was sorry
but no I was on my way to class and no I'm sorry
but I didn't have the time and there's nothing about you
that isn't lovely and shiny in the rain but no my car
is ugly and I'm not the man you think I am
but please Miss Botticelli please get out of the rain
(which I didn't actually say but could've).

So she smiled back with eyes that let nothing in or out
and I rolled up my window but didn't drive away
because as I said before we were all of us just stuck in
traffic on West 4th Street.

Short Days

(Autumn, 2001)

Sunday

Rake the leaves in Autumn,
on this day under this sun,
the angle of light precise
as a jet's aim. Catch the ball
my daughter throws, hope she
catches it before it rolls
to the street. Admire the birds
at the feeder, their consistency,
their tenacity. Admire too the stray
cat who watches the birds and waits.
Answer the phone before the fourth
ring, hear my wife's voice comfortably
near telling me what she's found
for the house. On my way back outside,
consider my own long slow death
years away, or the quick one
tomorrow. Later, buy one small thing
at the market, prepare the meat,
season the vegetables, open the wine.
And all day the television's game
deep in the background, strong men
throwing themselves at the dirt
over and over, precise as bombs
with love for their targets.
When the sun sets, grow sad,

and that sadness is my home.
Shut the doors, turn on the lights,
and wait for word of morning.

Monday

I linger in bed listening
to the city revive, a train
whose tracks throb all night.
I boil the water, eat the food,
read the paper that appeared
on my doorstep hours before:
Remembering the Victims. Open
the blinds, but not all the way.
Wake up hold me it's morning.
Build with this enterprise
something to live on, not just
routine, but a design, a method,
a plan to meet the day and therefore
every day, singularly and without
prejudice. An impossible task,
this constancy, but each day
calls for some economy.

Tuesday

Every Tuesday is the same,
each sunrise born of one event
merely infinitely repeated.
The sun lifts as surely
as the jet rises, a matter
of simple mechanics. Watch
again how the day breaks,
it breaks, and remember
how that jet on that day broke

the sky that held the steel
and glass, broke the air below.
*It was a place near my home,
the whole city my home,*
an old friend says on the phone.
And the men who took the plane
at half the speed of sound, burst
through that light: they too
understood the mechanics of the day.

Wednesday

From my bed I hear cars racing
in the street a block away,
the shriek of their tires waking me
from a dream that's already nearly gone.
I go to the window. The trees
are filled with mist, and this
is my reality: half awake,
half in the dream of waking,
stumbling in the night toward dawn
as the sound of car engines fade.
What was it? my wife asks,
and I say *I don't know.*
I kneel before the window and wait.
The street lies silent and damp,
leaves gathering in the gutters,
a faint smell of exhaust in the air.
When I wake up again, it will feel as if
I've come through something immense,
like birth or death,
but I'll be simply in my own bed.

Thursday

Today consider the leaves
and how they fall. The maple
quits early, splendidly, burning
from the inside out, and capitulates
with the extravagance of fire.
The sycamore throws down branch
and leaf alike while still green,
as if disaster was a way of life.
The oak smolders, and clings
to brown leaves deep into winter,
letting go only next spring.
Let me be the oak, patient
in the face of the season,
even if it takes forever.

Friday

It's as if seven short days
are all there is, and six
are spent waiting for the next.
Today it comes, that first frost
that kills all the delicate things
we planted months ago, and we're glad
to have it over with, confused
at our own pleasure in death,
yet somehow reassured or at least
awakened to the possibility
that for now we're safe.
See the beaten leaves?
Although I love them, I'm relieved
they are something other than me.

Saturday

After sleeping for an hour,
I wake up angry. I have forgotten
something important, and stumble
downstairs, turning on every
light in the house. The cat
trots after me, expecting to be fed.
Through the kitchen window
I see the backyard swing
careening in the wind.
Ignatow said that trees also
are depressed, but my sycamore
leans into the sky and takes
everything that comes.
There's nothing to be found
here tonight. I feed the cat,
pour a glass of water
and drink it slowly, then
turn off all the lights
and go back to bed.
This happens all year, until
one night when I look outside
the tree is gone. And there I am,
looking back in from the glass.

The Mouth of the Sea

Alone in a borrowed boat, my mother,
father, and I, we skimmed past parched fields ripe

with cicada, caught the current slowly,
saw dragonflies dip and land and land again,

always wavering, never stopping, never going.
The grass on the river bank spoke silence, and nothing

happened in the shape of the current that mattered
more than the touch of the paddles, those small pools and ripples,

the dimpling river carrying us away.
We shared the hollow silence of her absence.

There was nothing else to do.
We had to go on living a life of loss and sorrow,

and the boat and paddles were useless
for this journey. We thought the fields

and woods slipped slowly by, but they didn't,
you know. It was just us riding the torrent

that drives the stream that pushes the spinning, circling planet
until, at last, we reach the mouth of the sea.

Fast Water Past the Cheese House

On July 29, 1988, on a dry sunny day with the world spread out before it, my younger sister Amy Elizabeth was killed in a car crash on Route 27 in Edison, New Jersey when her roommate who was driving turned left into oncoming traffic. She died instantly. She was 20 years old. In that moment, and in the many moments that followed that summer and beyond, everything stuttered and skipped across my family's life and left us looking like the road on that corner on Route 27 in Edison, New Jersey, which was – as I came to see for myself a few months later – tattooed with innumerable swirling skid marks that told stories I'd never know or want to know.

In reaction to their daughter's death, my parents slowly closed themselves off from the world, like a film of a butterfly emerging from a chrysalis, but in reverse. In reaction to my sister's death, I found myself suddenly and inexplicably either cut in half or, paradoxically, doubled. Did I have only half my life left or was I somehow multiplied by the absence of her life? It's been 33 years and I've never been able to answer that question and I don't think it matters anymore.

My father had been a middle school teacher, and the year after Amy died, he retired and my parents left the house they'd lived in since 1964 – the house I grew up in, the house I still walk through in my dreams – and moved to a semi-desolate mountainside in Vermont. The move ticked all the metaphorical boxes: the new house had been abandoned by the previous owners and damaged by the hard Vermont winters; it was on a lot of land set back from the road with no indication of who lived there; they left all their living and dead relatives in New Jersey and moved to a neighborhood with no neighbors; the house was too large and difficult to keep warm so they shivered through the winters; the land itself was a wilderness of tall trees all the same age that had been growing since the last time the surrounding forest had been lumbered out.

The same year my parents moved to Vermont, my wife and I moved to from New Jersey to Ohio. What had once been an easy weekly dinner had suddenly become an arduous two-day drive. We were all of us marooned, at sea, stunned, drifting with the current. But there was no current.

We are not Vermonters. We are flatlanders from New Jersey. But Vermont was a fitting destination for my parents, in or out of crisis. We first went there in the summer of 1967, as a second vacation after our usual two weeks at the Jersey shore. My mother was three months pregnant with Amy. We stayed on the shores of Lake Dunmore, beneath Mt. Moosalamoo. I had never seen anything like this before: the lake, the mountain, the reflection of the mountain in the lake. It was all new. I paddled a canoe. I collected newts. In some very real way, I feel as if I've never left the shores of that lake on that summer morning while the water touched my fingers. My parents were similarly impressed. We kept coming back, driving up north in a series of used cars that sighed and sputtered but got us there. We drove past cows and barns and more cows and barns and fields, past old-fashioned roadside attractions and tiny one-star motels pressed up against the edges of Route 7. As the years passed, I knew to look for landmarks on the trip: The Portage Diner, the Bennington Monument, Jansen's, the Cheese House, Emerald Lake, and, most improbably in the heart of the Green Mountains, Seashell City, the pronunciation of which we intentionally bungled every time we saw it. And the towns along the way: Bennington, Manchester, Wallingford, Rutland, Pittsford, Brandon, Middlebury, and ultimately, Salisbury. Vermont was a place far from the exurban chaos of the Tri State area, it was a different country. So, my parents' return to the mountains and lakes and the mountains reflected in the lakes in a time of enormous need was understandable, even practical. Where do you go when there's no place to go?

My task that year was to continue to be their child while simultaneously being an adult who was also grieving a loss so huge and devastating that it sometimes seemed ridiculous: how could something so stupid happen? Of course things that stupid happen every day, all over the world, and I was no exception. You love someone, then they die. You love them because they'll die – something I'm not sure I really believe, but a sobering enough thought to catch you staring out the kitchen window at a winter dusk not turning on the lights while you fumble around with knives making dinner. My parents needed consolation but so did I. They needed presence. But I was too far away, in the middle of an unemployed corn field in Ohio.

Why was I in Ohio? My wife Wendy had picked up a one-semester appointment at Oberlin College, and since the job prospects of nearly-PhDs in English in the late '80s were limited in New Jersey, we put the cat in the Rabbit and rolled out west on Route 80. At first, it felt like an extended vacation, but when the job was renewed for another year and then another, we realized that Ohio might be more permanent than we thought. (Spoiler alert: I'm writing this in Ohio in 2023.) This was a time of our lives when we could still more or less flourish on thirty thousand dollars a year. I had a brief teaching gig fifty miles south at Wooster College, which fell flat when I corrected the department chair while explaining my take on dead metaphors, mainly that they weren't dead. My foremost memory of that job was the one-hour commute on the barely rolling farm roads of Wayne County, during which I'd wave to the Amish in their buggies and count the dead animals that collected in the ruts and ditches.

I was also running seventy miles a week, theoretically in training for a marathon I never ran, but I'll talk about that somewhere else. For now it's enough to admit that I was both punishing myself and pushing forward to a point on the horizon that kept receding.

My parents meanwhile had staked their claim on that semi-desolate mountainside and tried to tame the wilderness of grief. They cut down trees, mowed fallow fields, planted flowers, chopped wood, dug a pond, carried water to the pond. Their project was as boundless as the woods that surrounded them; they never ran out of things to plan. In short, there was no end in sight for any of us.

During the second summer in Ohio, I drove alone from that unemployed corn field to visit my parents on their semi-desolate mountainside in Vermont. After ten grueling hours, I pulled in their road before dark. We drank Jameson's and went to bed. The next day I planted flowers, mowed fields, chopped wood, looked out over the dark expanse of trees all the same height and told them we needed to get away for a few hours. "Wear your sloppy clothes," I said. We rented a canoe, were driven a few miles upstream, dropped off and given only one piece of advice from our guide, a young man with a long, full beard and a baseball cap: "There's fast water past the Cheese House." We solemnly nodded at this information, climbed into the boat and paddled away. I was in the stern, my father in the bow, and my mother sat between on a life preserver, dragging her hand through the water.

The Battenkill River begins in East Dorset and meanders for sixty miles through southern Vermont and New York State. It's a rocky, shallow stream, slow and quiet, with plenty of fish. Once it passes into New York, it widens as it's fed by more brooks and creeks, eventually flowing into the Hudson. The Hudson flows into the sea, but reluctantly. On this day, the plan was to paddle no more than ten miles, from Manchester, through Sunderland, past the Arlington covered bridge, to wait for our guide to pick us up. The trip would take three hours. We brought sandwiches. An hour in, my mother suddenly spoke: "What does 'fast water' mean?"

Two years earlier, a few months after the accident, while we were all still living in New Jersey, my father and I had to make our way to the Middlesex County courthouse for a deposition that would ultimately lead to a trial to determine the worth of Amy's life for the insurance companies involved. (This trial was a miserable and excruciating affair that left everyone angry, bitter, and sobbing. I'll say nothing else about it.) Before the trip, we had made a solemn and mostly silent pledge to each other: find the corner of Route 27 in Edison, New Jersey where the accident had taken place. It was my father's idea, and I assented mindlessly. Route 27 begins in Newark and ends in Princeton, with all the major stops in between. Once part of the Lincoln Highway, it's a messy and ill-kept corridor that's lined with continuous strip malls, strip clubs, and garages, doglegging through once-quaint small towns that succumbed to exurban spread fifty years ago. We approached from the north, moving too slow for the traffic around us, dodging the semis, stopping every mile at a traffic light. At that intersection in Edison, we pulled over, got out of the car, and stepped into a dense New Jersey blanket of dry September heat.

We had no idea what to do, but it didn't involve talk. I knew only one thing – somehow, I had a right to be here. This patch of land, this asphalt hell scarred and warped with the limitless grind of wheel on earth, wheel on wheel, metal on metal, this was somehow mine. I stood in the heat and expected nothing. I crossed the street and saw what I saw. I stood on the curb and looked down at the black and tarry ground and felt nothing. I waited but I didn't wait. At the edge of my vision was a thing. There, next to the curb, next to storm drain at the edge of the street, there. A shoe. Pale green leather, flimsy, thin-soled and filthy. I picked it up. I looked at it, a conjunction of time and place and circumstance. I was holding Amy's right shoe, the match to the one on her left foot she was wearing in the ambulance, in the emergency room, in the morgue. It was the missing shoe and I had found it. I had found it, and it was nothing and it was everything.

Fast water means that the water is fast. Not white water, which foams and bubbles. This is the Battenkill, not the Colorado. It's an ordinary stream in a safe New England county, surrounded by more living things than you could ever wish for. When the water is fast, that means it's faster than the water before it. When you can see the Cheese House – perched up on a small spit of land between Route 7A and the Battenkill, between Sunderland and Arlington – then the water will be faster than it was before. Steering in the stern, I could see how the river dipped and spread, the broad ripples that cut from bank to bank. I knew to aim for the flattest expanse of water and hope for the best. Through the trees, I saw the yellow

Cheese House up the bank on my left. The canoe shuddered, then surged forward. For one moment, we were suspended at the crest of an eddy, then dropped slowly into the river, softly stopping on a sand bar. The canoe pivoted on an invisible fulcrum, and we helplessly spun a quarter turn to the right. We were grounded. I sat for a moment. There was only one thing to do. "Everybody out," I said. And we stepped into the swirling current up to our knees, dragged and hauled the canoe from its place on the sandbar, climbed back in and continued downstream to the Arlington Covered Bridge, where our guide was waiting to bring us home.

Acknowledgements

"Mad Tom" names a brook, road, mountain, notch, and orchard in East Dorset, Vermont.

"Nancy & Me & the Men in the Moon" and "The Brick Path" appeared in Typehouse, Vol 8 number 3 Issue 23. Versions of "Misreading Keats" and "Garbage" appeared in the Modern Poetry Quarterly Review, Issue 12. "Kestrel" and "Nothing Falling" appeared in the Modern Poetry Quarterly Review, Issue 14. "The Cowbird" appeared in Poetry Wales Interviews 11.9.22. "Solstice" appeared in Italian Americana Vol 40, number 2. "Road Kills" and "Mr. Hard…" appeared in The Muddy River Review, Issue 27. An earlier version of "Sonnet on the Night John Lennon Dies" appeared in Ovunque Siamo, Autumn 2022. "Pinking" and "The Red Salamander" appeared in Sheila-Na-Gig Spring 2023. "The Words Not Included in This Poem" appeared in Feral #17, September 2023. "Short Days" appeared in Voices in Italian Americana (VIA) 34.2, 2023. "Finding My Religion" appeared in Verse Virtual, March 2024. "On the Great Wall," "Pareidolia," and "Crow" appeared in Verse Virtual, October 2024.

About the Author

MATTHEW CARIELLO is the author of four poetry collections: two of the poetry collections, *A Boat That Can Carry Two* (2011) and *Talk* (2019) were published by Bordighera Press. *The Empty Field* was published in 2022 by Red Moon Press; *Self Portrait in the Dark* was published in 2025 by Finishing Line Press. He is a senior lecturer in the English department at The Ohio State University in Columbus.

VIA FOLIOS
A refereed book series dedicated to the culture of Italians and Italian Americans.

GRACE CAVALIERI. *Fables from Italy and Beyond.* Vol. 178. Poetry.
LAURETTE FOLK. *Eleison.* Vol. 177. Novel.
FRANCES NEVILL. *Coquina Soup.* Vol. 176. Literature.
FRANCINE MASIELLO. *The Tomb of the Divers.* Vol. 175. Novel.
PIETRO DI DONATO. *Collected Stories.* Vol. 174. Literature.
RACHEL GUIDO deVRIES. *The Birthday Years.* Vol. 173. Poetry.
MATTHEW MEDURI. *Collegiate Gothic.* Vol. 172. Novel.
THOMAS RUGGIO. *Finding Dandini.* Vol. 171. Art History.
TAMBURRI GIORDANO GARDAPHÈ. *From the Margin.* Vol. 170. Anthology.
ANNA MONARDO. *After Italy.* Vol. 169. Memoir.
JOEY NICOLETTI. *Extinction Wednesday.* Vol. 168. Poetry.
MARIA FAMÀ. *Trigger.* Vol. 167. Poetry.
WILLI Q MINN. *What? Nothing.* Vol. 166. Poetry.
RICHARD VETERE. *She's Not There.* Vol. 165. Literature.
FRANK GIOIA. *Mercury Man.* Vol. 164. Literature.
LUISA M. GIULIANETTI. *Agrodolce.* Vol. 163. Literature.
ANGELO ZEOLLA. *The Bronx Unbound ovvero i versi bronxesi.* Vol. 162. Poetry.
NICHOLAS A. DiCHARIO. *Giovanni's Tree.* Vol. 161. Literature.
ADELE ANNESI. *What She Takes Away.* Vol. 160. Novel.
ANNIE RACHELE LANZILLOTTO. *Whaddyacall the Wind?.* Vol. 159. Memoir.
JULIA LISELLA. *Our Lively Kingdom.* Vol. 158. Poetry.
MARK CIABATTARI. *When the Mask Slips.* Vol. 157. Novel.
JENNIFER MARTELLI. *The Queen of Queens.* Vol. 156. Poetry.
TONY TADDEI. *The Sons of the Santorelli.* Vol. 155. Literature.
FRANCO RICCI. *Preston Street • Corso Italias.* Vol. 154. History.
MIKE FIORITO. *The Hated Ones.* Vol. 153. Literature.
PATRICIA DUNN. *Last Stop on the 6.* Vol. 152. Novel.
WILLIAM BOELHOWER. *Immigrant Autobiography.* Vol. 151. Literary Criticism.
MARC DIPAOLO. *Fake Italian.* Vol. 150. Literature.
GAIL REITANO. *Italian Love Cake.* Vol. 149. Novel.
VINCENT PANELLA. *Sicilian Dreams.* Vol. 148. Novel.
MARK CIABATTARI. *The Literal Truth: Rizzoli Dreams of Eating the Apple of Earthly Delights.* Vol. 147. Novel.
MARK CIABATTARI. *Dreams of An Imaginary New Yorker Named Rizzoli.* Vol. 146. Novel.
LAURETTE FOLK. *The End of Aphrodite.* Vol. 145. Novel.
ANNA CITRINO. *A Space Between.* Vol. 144. Poetry
MARIA FAMÀ. *The Good for the Good.* Vol. 143. Poetry.
ROSEMARY CAPPELLO. *Wonderful Disaster.* Vol. 142. Poetry.
B. AMORE. *Journeys on the Wheel.* Vol. 141. Poetry.
ALDO PALAZZESCHI. *The Manifestos of Aldo Palazzeschi.* Vol 140. Literature.
ROSS TALARICO. *The Reckoning.* Vol 139. Poetry.

MICHELLE REALE. *Season of Subtraction*. Vol 138. Poetry.
MARISA FRASCA. *Wild Fennel*. Vol 137. Poetry.
RITA ESPOSITO WATSON. *Italian Kisses*. Vol. 136. Memoir.
SARA FRUNER. *Bitter Bites from Sugar Hills*. Vol. 135. Poetry.
KATHY CURTO. *Not for Nothing*. Vol. 134. Memoir.
JENNIFER MARTELLI. *My Tarantella*. Vol. 133. Poetry.
MARIA TERRONE. *At Home in the New World*. Vol. 132. Essays.
GIL FAGIANI. *Missing Madonnas*. Vol. 131. Poetry.
LEWIS TURCO. *The Sonnetarium*. Vol. 130. Poetry.
JOE AMATO. *Samuel Taylor's Hollywood Adventure*. Vol. 129. Novel.
BEA TUSIANI. *Con Amore*. Vol. 128. Memoir.
MARIA GIURA. *What My Father Taught Me*. Vol. 127. Poetry.
STANISLAO PUGLIESE. *A Century of Sinatra*. Vol. 126. Popular Culture.
TONY ARDIZZONE. *The Arab's Ox*. Vol. 125. Novel.
PHYLLIS CAPELLO. *Packs Small Plays Big*. Vol. 124. Literature.
FRED GARDAPHÉ. *Read 'em and Reap*. Vol. 123. Criticism.
JOSEPH A. AMATO. *Diagnostics*. Vol 122. Literature.
DENNIS BARONE. *Second Thoughts*. Vol 121. Poetry.
OLIVIA K. CERRONE. *The Hunger Saint*. Vol 120. Novella.
GARIBLADI M. LAPOLLA. *Miss Rollins in Love*. Vol 119. Novel.
JOSEPH TUSIANI. *A Clarion Call*. Vol 118. Poetry.
JOSEPH A. AMATO. *My Three Sicilies*. Vol 117. Poetry & Prose.
MARGHERITA COSTA. *Voice of a Virtuosa and Coutesan*. Vol 116. Poetry.
NICOLE SANTALUCIA. *Because I Did Not Die*. Vol 115. Poetry.
MARK CIABATTARI. *Preludes to History*. Vol 114. Poetry.
HELEN BAROLINI. *Visits*. Vol 113. Novel.
ERNESTO LIVORNI. *The Fathers' America*. Vol. 112. Poetry.
MARIO B. MIGNONE. *The Story of My People*. Vol 111. Non-fiction.
GEORGE GUIDA. *The Sleeping Gulf*. Vol 110. Poetry.
JOEY NICOLETTI. *Reverse Graffiti*. Vol 109. Poetry.
GIOSE RIMANELLI. *Il mestiere del furbo*. Vol 108. Criticism.
LEWIS TURCO. *The Hero Enkidu*. Vol. 107. Poetry.
AL TACCONELLI. *Perhaps Fly*. Vol 106. Poetry.
RACHEL GUIDO DEVRIES. *A Woman Unknown in Her Bones*. Vol 105. Poetry.
BERNARD BRUNO. *A Tear and a Tear in My Heart*. Vol 104. Non-fiction.
FELIX STEFANILE. *Songs of the Sparrow*. Vol. 103. Poetry.
FRANK POLIZZI. *A New Life with Bianca*. Vol 102. Poetry.
GIL FAGIANI. *Stone Walls*. Vol 101. Poetry.
LOUISE DESALVO. *Casting Off*. Vol 100. Fiction.
MARY JO BONA. *I Stop Waiting for You*. Vol 99. Poetry.
RACHEL GUIDO DEVRIES. *Stati zitt, Josie*. Vol 98. Children's Literature. $8
GRACE CAVALIERI. *The Mandate of Heaven*. Vol 97. Poetry.
MARISA FRASCA. *Via incanto*. Vol 96. Poetry.
DOUGLAS GLADSTONE. *Carving a Niche for Himself*. Vol 95. History.
MARIA TERRONE. *Eye to Eye*. Vol 94. Poetry.
CONSTANCE SANCETTA. *Here in Cerchio*. Vol 93. Local History.

MARIA MAZZIOTTI GILLAN. *Ancestors' Song*. Vol 92. Poetry.
MICHAEL PARENTI. *Waiting for Yesterday: Pages from a Street Kid's Life*. Vol 90. Memoir.
ANNIE LANZILLOTTO. *Schistsong*. Vol 89. Poetry.
EMANUEL DI PASQUALE. *Love Lines*. Vol 88. Poetry.
CAROSONE & LOGIUDICE. *Our Naked Lives*. Vol 87. Essays.
JAMES PERICONI. *Strangers in a Strange Land: A Survey of Italian-Language American Books*.Vol 86. Book History.
DANIELA GIOSEFFI. *Escaping La Vita Della Cucina*. Vol 85. Essays.
MARIA FAMÀ. *Mystics in the Family*. Vol 84. Poetry.
ROSSANA DEL ZIO. *From Bread and Tomatoes to Zuppa di Pesce "Ciambotto"*. Vol. 83. Memoir.
LORENZO DELBOCA. *Polentoni*. Vol 82. Italian Studies.
SAMUEL GHELLI. *A Reference Grammar*. Vol 81. Italian Language.
ROSS TALARICO. *Sled Run*. Vol 80. Fiction.
FRED MISURELLA. *Only Sons*. Vol 79. Fiction.
FRANK LENTRICCHIA. *The Portable Lentricchia*. Vol 78. Fiction.
RICHARD VETERE. *The Other Colors in a Snow Storm*. Vol 77. Poetry.
GARIBALDI LAPOLLA. *Fire in the Flesh*. Vol 76 Fiction & Criticism.
GEORGE GUIDA. *The Pope Stories*. Vol 75 Prose.
ROBERT VISCUSI. *Ellis Island*. Vol 74. Poetry.
ELENA GIANINI BELOTTI. *The Bitter Taste of Strangers Bread*. Vol 73. Fiction.
PINO APRILE. *Terroni*. Vol 72. Italian Studies.
EMANUEL DI PASQUALE. *Harvest*. Vol 71. Poetry.
ROBERT ZWEIG. *Return to Naples*. Vol 70. Memoir.
AIROS & CAPPELLI. *Guido*. Vol 69. Italian/American Studies.
FRED GARDAPHÉ. *Moustache Pete is Dead! Long Live Moustache Pete!*. Vol 67. Literature/Oral History.
PAOLO RUFFILLI. *Dark Room/Camera oscura*. Vol 66. Poetry.
HELEN BAROLINI. *Crossing the Alps*. Vol 65. Fiction.
COSMO FERRARA. *Profiles of Italian Americans*. Vol 64. Italian Americana.
GIL FAGIANI. *Chianti in Connecticut*. Vol 63. Poetry.
BASSETTI & D'ACQUINO. *Italic Lessons*. Vol 62. Italian/American Studies.
CAVALIERI & PASCARELLI, Eds. *The Poet's Cookbook*. Vol 61. Poetry/Recipes.
EMANUEL DI PASQUALE. *Siciliana*. Vol 60. Poetry.
NATALIA COSTA, Ed. *Bufalini*. Vol 59. Poetry.
RICHARD VETERE. *Baroque*. Vol 58. Fiction.
LEWIS TURCO. *La Famiglia/The Family*. Vol 57. Memoir.
NICK JAMES MILETI. *The Unscrupulous*. Vol 56. Humanities.
BASSETTI. ACCOLLA. D'AQUINO. *Italici: An Encounter with Piero Bassetti*. Vol 55. Italian Studies.
GIOSE RIMANELLI. *The Three-legged One*. Vol 54. Fiction.
CHARLES KLOPP. *Bele Antiche Stòrie*. Vol 53. Criticism.
JOSEPH RICAPITO. *Second Wave*. Vol 52. Poetry.
GARY MORMINO. *Italians in Florida*. Vol 51. History.
GIANFRANCO ANGELUCCI. *Federico F*. Vol 50. Fiction.

ANTHONY VALERIO. *The Little Sailor*. Vol 49. Memoir.
ROSS TALARICO. *The Reptilian Interludes*. Vol 48. Poetry.
RACHEL GUIDO DE VRIES. *Teeny Tiny Tino's Fishing Story*.
   Vol 47. Children's Literature.
EMANUEL DI PASQUALE. *Writing Anew*. Vol 46. Poetry.
MARIA FAMÀ. *Looking For Cover*. Vol 45. Poetry.
ANTHONY VALERIO. *Toni Cade Bambara's One Sicilian Night*. Vol 44. Poetry.
EMANUEL CARNEVALI. *Furnished Rooms*. Vol 43. Poetry.
BRENT ADKINS. et al., Ed. *Shifting Borders. Negotiating Places*.
   Vol 42. Conference.
GEORGE GUIDA. *Low Italian*. Vol 41. Poetry.
GARDAPHÈ, GIORDANO, TAMBURRI. *Introducing Italian Americana*.
   Vol 40. Italian/American Studies.
DANIELA GIOSEFFI. *Blood Autumn/Autunno di sangue*. Vol 39. Poetry.
FRED MISURELLA. *Lies to Live By*. Vol 38. Stories.
STEVEN BELLUSCIO. *Constructing a Bibliography*. Vol 37. Italian Americana.
ANTHONY JULIAN TAMBURRI, Ed. *Italian Cultural Studies 2002*.
   Vol 36. Essays.
BEA TUSIANI. *con amore*. Vol 35. Memoir.
FLAVIA BRIZIO-SKOV, Ed. *Reconstructing Societies in the Aftermath of War*.
   Vol 34. History.
TAMBURRI. et al., Eds. *Italian Cultural Studies 2001*. Vol 33. Essays.
ELIZABETH G. MESSINA, Ed. *In Our Own Voices*.
   Vol 32. Italian/American Studies.
STANISLAO G. PUGLIESE. *Desperate Inscriptions*. Vol 31. History.
HOSTERT & TAMBURRI, Eds. *Screening Ethnicity*.
   Vol 30. Italian/American Culture.
G. PARATI & B. LAWTON, Eds. *Italian Cultural Studies*. Vol 29. Essays.
HELEN BAROLINI. *More Italian Hours*. Vol 28. Fiction.
FRANCO NASI, Ed. *Intorno alla Via Emilia*. Vol 27. Culture.
ARTHUR L. CLEMENTS. *The Book of Madness & Love*. Vol 26. Poetry.
JOHN CASEY, et al. *Imagining Humanity*. Vol 25. Interdisciplinary Studies.
ROBERT LIMA. *Sardinia/Sardegna*. Vol 24. Poetry.
DANIELA GIOSEFFI. *Going On*. Vol 23. Poetry.
ROSS TALARICO. *The Journey Home*. Vol 22. Poetry.
EMANUEL DI PASQUALE. *The Silver Lake Love Poems*. Vol 21. Poetry.
JOSEPH TUSIANI. *Ethnicity*. Vol 20. Poetry.
JENNIFER LAGIER. *Second Class Citizen*. Vol 19. Poetry.
FELIX STEFANILE. *The Country of Absence*. Vol 18. Poetry.
PHILIP CANNISTRARO. *Blackshirts*. Vol 17. History.
LUIGI RUSTICHELLI, Ed. *Seminario sul racconto*. Vol 16. Narrative.
LEWIS TURCO. *Shaking the Family Tree*. Vol 15. Memoirs.
LUIGI RUSTICHELLI, Ed. *Seminario sulla drammaturgia*.
   Vol 14. Theater/Essays.
FRED GARDAPHÈ. *Moustache Pete is Dead! Long Live Moustache Pete!*.
   Vol 13. Oral Literature.

JONE GAILLARD CORSI. *Il libretto d'autore. 1860 - 1930*. Vol 12. Criticism.
HELEN BAROLINI. *Chiaroscuro: Essays of Identity*. Vol 11. Essays.
PICARAZZI & FEINSTEIN, Eds. *An African Harlequin in Milan*.
  Vol 10. Theater/Essays.
JOSEPH RICAPITO. *Florentine Streets & Other Poems*. Vol 9. Poetry.
FRED MISURELLA. *Short Time*. Vol 8. Novella.
NED CONDINI. *Quartettsatz*. Vol 7. Poetry.
ANTHONY JULIAN TAMBURRI, Ed. *Fuori: Essays by Italian/American Lesbiansand Gays*. Vol 6. Essays.
ANTONIO GRAMSCI. P. Verdicchio. Trans. & Intro. *The Southern Question*.
  Vol 5. Social Criticism.
DANIELA GIOSEFFI. *Word Wounds & Water Flowers*. Vol 4. Poetry. $8
WILEY FEINSTEIN. *Humility's Deceit: Calvino Reading Ariosto Reading Calvino*.
  Vol 3. Criticism.
PAOLO A. GIORDANO, Ed. *Joseph Tusiani: Poet. Translator. Humanist*.
  Vol 2. Criticism.
ROBERT VISCUSI. *Oration Upon the Most Recent Death of Christopher Columbus*.
  Vol 1. Poetry.

www.ingramcontent.com/pod-product-compliance
Lightning Source LLC
Chambersburg PA
CBHW022119090426
42743CB00008B/918